D1135538

# I'VE LIVED IN EAST LONDON
# FOR 86½ YEARS

*Words by Joseph Markovitch*
*Photographs by Martin Usborne*

HOXTON MINI PRESS

*I've Lived in East London for 86½ Years*
Fourth Edition

Copyright © Martin Usborne 2013. All rights reserved.

Photography by Martin Usborne
Words by Joseph Markovitch
Design and layout by Martin Usborne and Friederike Huber
Series design by breadcollective.co.uk

A CIP catalogue record for this book is available from the British Library.

ISBN: 978-0-9576998-0-9

First published in the United Kingdom in 2013 by Hoxton Mini Press
Reprinted in 2014 & 2015.

No part of this publication may be reproduced, stored in a retrieval system,
or transmitted in any form or by any means, electronic, mechanical,
photocopying, recording or otherwise, without the prior written permission
of the copyright owner.

Printed and bound by WKT, China

To order books, collector's editions and signed prints please go to
www.hoxtonminipress.com

*East London Photo Stories:*

*Book One*

*Also in this series:*

*Book Two*
East London Swimmers

*Book Three*
A Portrait of Hackney

*Books and signed prints available at:*

**www.hoxtonminipress.com**

# INTRODUCTION

Summer 2007, mid-day. There he was in Hoxton Square standing with plastic bag in hand, oversized blazer slipping off his shoulders, chatting to various neon-clad youth lying in the sun. I assumed Joseph was lost or homeless or possibly a little mad. I assumed he might have alcohol in his bag. I was wrong on all accounts. It turned out that he, more than any of us young pretenders, was rooted in this area and was much more sane than all of us. For eighty years Joe had witnessed a continual cultural transformation that we could only imagine: where he knew cabinetmakers, we knew cocktail bars, where he frequented music halls, we walked past modern estates. In his plastic bag he carried what he always carried - a small carton of orange squash.

Over the next few months Joe was kind enough to let me photograph him around the streets and in his home. I planned to make a book about the history of this rich and diverse area. Joe, however, wanted to talk about action movies, tall Scandinavian women, Nicolas Cage, the catarrh congesting his chest and how technology might blow up the world. Joe had never once left England, and rarely London, but his vibrant imagination – aided by books from various Hackney libraries and popular magazines – had enabled him to travel through virtual Amazonian rainforests and into the dark jungles of celebrities' private lives.

This book is an updated version of what was originally intended to be a small pamphlet to accompany an exhibition of these images. To my surprise the pamphlet sold out quickly and the following editions of the book - paperback, then thin hardback, then slightly less-thin harback - created small profits that allowed Joe to buy two phones, a DVD player, a new digital TV, two coats, a batch of winter socks, a new belt, a digital radio and, crucially, a number of Clarks shoes for his long walks around East London. The pleasure of making this book with Joe then prompted the start of *Hoxton Mini Press*, a small publishing company about East London of which this is the first book. Thank you to all of you who have made this possible.

In early 2013 Joseph's life changed drastically. His health deteriorated and he was forced to move out of East London. He always told me that he hated homes for the elderly ('They throw away the key they do') but after many hospital visits he reluctantly accepted permanent help. With his reduced ability to walk his mental journeys became less far-reaching too and he said he no longer wanted to visit the Amazon ('Deep in the jungle is no good for people with a bad chest'). Joseph's life was utterly bound to the neighborhoods of Shoreditch and Bethnal Green. That is where he was born, where he grew up, where he lived. As the area transformed, his shuffling walk and slightly too-short trousers remained a constant. When he was forced to move it was the beginning of his end.

On December 26th, 2013, a few days short of his 87th birthday, Joseph passed away. Not long after, on an unusually sunny winter's day, his small coffin was lowered into the ground at a Jewish cemetery just east of London and I helped throw a few clumps of soil into the grave.

Joseph lived a quiet but rich life. During his final days in hospital he was visited by both a pastor and a rabbi much to the confusion of the nursing staff. Joseph considered himself Jewish but frequently went to the church because he liked the people and the sandwiches. Perhaps he left us with a smile, enjoying the best of both worlds. I hope so because his final days were painful for both his mind and his body.

After the funeral I met Joseph's nephew, a man called

Anthony, who later sent me a photo of Joseph aged 16 which is now at the end of this book. I love this picture - I see his whole life in those eyes, perhaps because his expression seems almost identical to how it appeared to me some 70 years later.

Joseph was an unusual friend to me – in some ways I knew him intimately, in other ways not at all. He spoke with a deep honesty but his tales and ideas were often from a distant galaxy. And yet, across that divide, one thing was immediately clear: he was a kind man.

I used to think that the process of growing old was a gentle retreat into darkness rather like a spent actor leaving the stage backwards, stumbling at the last. Joe has shown me something of the light – and lightness – of old age. Even though his recent story has been painful, I only hope that I also age into someone as colourful and as open-hearted as Joe.

To Joseph Markovitch, with gratitude,

Martin Usborne,
*Hackney, London, July 2014*

## ON CHILDHOOD

I was born right by Old Street roundabout on January 1st, 1927. Some of the kids used to beat me up – but in a friendly way. Hoxton was full of characters in those days. The Mayor was called Mr. Brooks and he was also a chimney sweep. Guess what? Before the Coronation, he was putting up decorations and he fell off a ladder and got killed. Well, it happens. Then there was a six-foot-tall girl, she was really massive. She used to attack people and put them in police vans. Maria was her name. Then there was Brotsky who used to kill chickens with a long stick. His son's name was Monty. That's not a common one is it? 'Monty Brotsky'.

A lot of young kids do graffiti around Hoxton ...

... it's nice. It adds a bit of colour, don't you think?

## ON FASHION

In the old days, when a man went to see the opera he had on a bowler hat. If you were a man and you walked in the street without a hat on your head you were a lost soul. People don't wear hats any more... but they wear everything else, don't they?

## ON RELATIONSHIPS

I've never had a girlfriend. It's better that way. I've always had very bad catarrh so it wasn't possible. And I had to care for my mother. Anyway, if I was married I would have been domineered all my life by a girl and that ain't good for nobody's health. You know that Bernie Ecclestone, from Formula One, he is really, really small. He was married to a Serbian girl who was six-foot-one. I say 'lucky Bernie'. People always say that dark-haired girls like millionaires. My preference is very tall blonde Scandinavians. If they are Hispanic and really tall then I might just like them with dark hair. I would have liked to have had a girlfriend but its OK. I've seen the horse and cart, I've seen the camera invented, I've seen the projector. I never starved, that's the main thing.

## ON WORK

I worked two years as a Cabinet maker in Hemsworth Street just off Hoxton market. But when my sinuses got bad I went to Hackney Road putting rivets on luggage cases. For about twenty years I did that job. My foreman was a bastard. Apart from that it was OK. But if I was clever, very clever, then I would have liked to be an accountant. It's a very good job. And if I was less heavy... you know what I'd like to be? I'd like to be a ballet dancer. That would be my dream.

## ON THE UNIVERSE

What about those people that study the stars? That's a very good job. I'm interested in the universe. It's more interesting than rivets. If we sent a camera far enough into space we might see people with mouths in their necks and hearts in their heads. But the universe is a mystery, ain't it? How did silver happen, how did copper happen, how did coffee begin? No one knows. The first thing that brought light was candles. Hey, if a meteor landed in Hoxton square you think anyone could survive? Probably not.

## ON ART

I find all this modern art very strange. I'm not used to things I don't understand, things what ain't paintings. I like the old paintings. I'm interested in Renaissance – you know what that is? Things what are ancient. Anything between one hundred and three hundred years old. I also like things that are produced by Picasso, people like that. Toulouse-Lautrec. He was not too bad, but he had an unhappy life. Hey, do you know that Tracy Emin? She lives around here. You know that she stopped a skyscraper being built in Hoxton square. I'd like to meet her.

## ON THE OLYMPICS

We used to have cabinet makers and tailors and music halls. Now we have a big stadium. I'm not sure about it.

## ON HIS MOTHER

My mother was a good cook. She made bread pudding. It was the best pudding you could have. She was called Janie and I lived with her until she died. I wasn't going to let her into a home. Your mother should be your best friend. Our best memories were going on a Sunday to Hampstead Heath fair. There was a parrot there who used to swear at me. I once had a locket with a photo in it of my mother. I had to move house a few times and it went missing. There's no photos of her anymore. This is the shape of her locket, it was almost round.

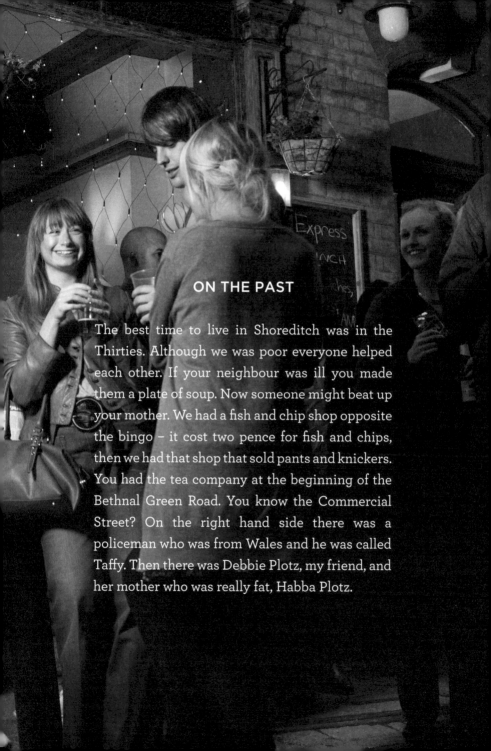

## ON THE PAST

The best time to live in Shoreditch was in the Thirties. Although we was poor everyone helped each other. If your neighbour was ill you made them a plate of soup. Now someone might beat up your mother. We had a fish and chip shop opposite the bingo – it cost two pence for fish and chips, then we had that shop that sold pants and knickers. You had the tea company at the beginning of the Bethnal Green Road. You know the Commercial Street? On the right hand side there was a policeman who was from Wales and he was called Taffy. Then there was Debbie Plotz, my friend, and her mother who was really fat, Habba Plotz.

## ON MONEY

I don't know what I would do if I won the lottery. There is that children's charity, what's it called? I wouldn't help them because they say the money goes straight to the terrorists. If I won a small amount of money I would give it to the Synagogue Burial Society – because I've got to pay for my own funeral. I've been paying into it for 35 years but every year they raise the prices. I could have buried a football team by now.

## ON READING

I like to go to the library on Monday, Tuesday and
... well, I can't always promise what days I go. I like
to read about places in the world. I also read a
book called *The Life of Stars*. Do you know Nicolas
Cage? He is half German and half Italian. The
problem is that nowadays you have to get a girl in
to bed to be a star. All the girls are dressed scantily
now, ain't it? Audrey Hepburn never dressed
scantily. James Cagney never was about sleeping
with the girls. What about that Joe Pesci? Where
are his parents from? I should look it up.

## ON RELIGION

I don't believe in God. But there must have been an explosion of some kind. Otherwise how did it all happen? The sky, moon, women, cats... I'm Jewish but I go to the Christian church because the people are nice. We see movies together. Last week we saw *Piranha 3D*. If Jesus had a camera the world would have been different. There might not have been wars because there would be evidence that all his miracles are true. But our brains were too small in those days to invent a camera. Shame.

## ON SADNESS

There's no point crying about things, is there? People don't see you when you're sad. Best just to keep walking.

## ON ETHNIC DIVERSITY

When I was a kid everyone was a cockney. Now it's a real mix. I makes it more interesting. Did you know that I stand still when I get trouble with my chest? Well, last Saturday a woman come up to me and said, 'Are you OK?' and I said, 'Why?' She said, 'Because you are standing still', I said 'Oh'. She said she comes from Italy and her husband is Scots-Canadian, and you know what? She wanted to help me! Then I dropped a twenty-pound note on a bus. A foreign man – I think he was Dutch or French said, 'You've dropped a twenty pound note.' English people don't do that because they have betting habits. They take your twenty-pound and go put it on the horses. What about Irish girls getting married to Chinamen in Liverpool! Crazy stuff.

## ON WALKING

I like to walk because I see things that I would
never see, like boats and ships and strange
people's faces. I would like to walk in the rainforest
but I'd have to be careful of the snakes and the
spiders, it's very dense over there. To get from
where I am standing now to the other side of that
wall would take you about an hour and a half. Did
you know that somewhere in the rainforest there
is a cure for all the bad diseases in the world but
the governments don't want to spend. I'd probably
live in a hut out there.

## ON JENNIFER LOPEZ

What about that singer? That Lopez girl. She's Puerto Rican. She can't be English with a name like Lopez. If she was born in Hoxton she would be called Jennifer Smith and that wouldn't be right. I think it's great that people are all mixed up. The most important thing is to be kind to each other.

## ON HOMOSEXUALITY (AND LETTUCE)

I didn't know what a homosexual was when I was young. Now there are homosexuals in the army. I think it's good – they don't desert on anyone. The only time I would ever be prejudiced is if someone stole my bread away. But I wouldn't do anything about it. That's the government's job to get involved. Do you know that I can't eat lettuce? I've got no teeth, not for ten years. It's hard to like lettuce if you haven't got no teeth.

## ON DOGS

I met a woman who had a dog. The dog was my friend almost straight away. That's because I didn't move my hands. Dogs know that about me, I never move my hands. Dogs have intuition. They can tell a bad person from a good person.

## ON HUMOUR

Lots of things make me laugh. Fruit makes me laugh. To see a dog talking makes me laugh. I like to see monkeys throwing coconuts on men's heads, that's funny. When you see a man going on to a desert island and he is stranded the monkeys are always friendly. You think the monkey is throwing things at your head but really he is throwing the coconuts for you to eat.

## ON CINEMA

All the best films were German. There was one with Peter Lorre and it was called *M*. He went about murdering children in Düsseldorf and the blind man finds him because he whistles. Germans also made sexy films. If you see *Dante's Inferno* they were all naked in that. I saw *The Sixth Sense*. That's funny. Everyone was dead! Hey, do you know something? Hitchcock used to make films around this part of town.

## ON TECHNOLOGY

Computers can start wars if you're not careful. You press the wrong button and a bomb goes off. In my time, if a woman wrote on a typewriter and she pressed the wrong key she just took the paper out and put it in the basket. Now you press a button and the whole economy collapses. There is all different computers. There are ones that send satellites up in the air. They are really complicated. But the ones that you get at home – they are just designed to get your bills on. The Microsoft ones, they are harder to use. If they are in the hands of a madman they can be really dangerous.

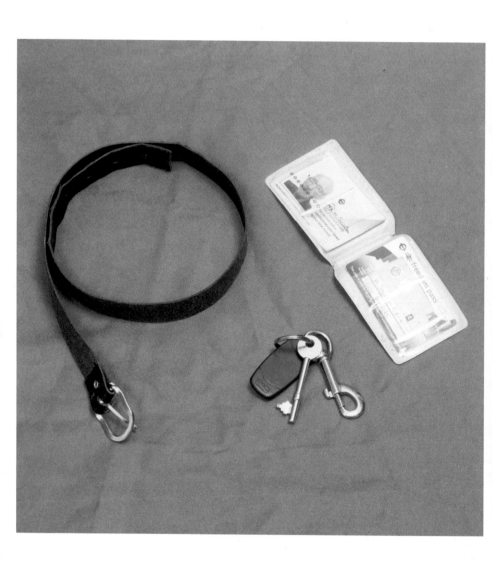

## ON THE MOST IMPORTANT THINGS IN LIFE

The most important thing I own is my keys. And my bus pass. And my belt. If you lose a cigarette or a pound coin you replace it. But if you lose your keys then you're left outside. And you can't get home because you've got no bus pass. And they won't let you on the bus if your trousers have fallen down. This is important stuff, you know.

## ON HEALTH

It's very painful getting older. My neck hurts all the time and I can't walk so easy. If I was rich or if I was a queen they would give me all these things to make it go away. They would save me. Nurse! Nurse! Where is everyone here? The corridors are totally empty. And there's no left or right to these hospital beds, only the middle. When I sleep I gotta have all of covered just like this. Why do I like to not see anything?

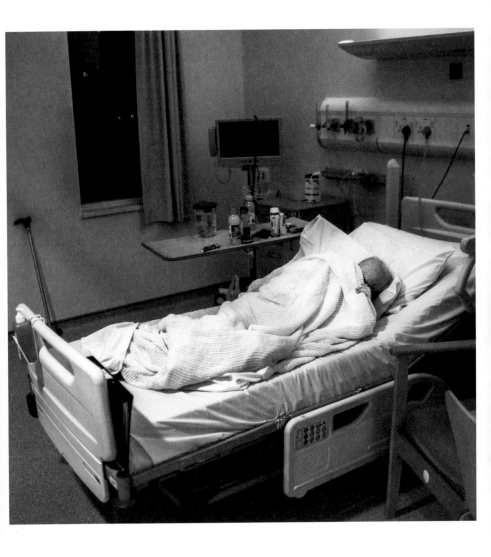

## ON THE FUTURE

If I try, I can imagine the future. It's like watching a film. Pavements will move, nurses will be robots and cars will get smaller and grow wings... you've just got to wait. They will make photographs that talk. You will look at a picture of me and you will hear me say: 'Hello, I'm Joseph Markovitch' and then it will be me telling you about things. Imagine that! I also have an idea that in about fifty years Hoxton Square will have a new market with an amazing plastic rain-cover. So if it rains the potatoes won't get wet. I don't know what else they will sell. Maybe bowler hats. Nothing much changes around here in the end.

*Aged 16, 1943*

JOSEPH MARKOVITCH

01.01.1927 - 26.12.2013